REFUSE TO DISAPPEAR

Also by Tara Betts:

*Break the Habit*
*Arc & Hue*

# REFUSE TO DISAPPEAR

*Tara Betts*

SELECTED BY CYNTHIA ARRIEU-KING
FOR THE HILARY THAM CAPITAL COLLECTION
BRAD RICHARD, SERIES EDITOR

· THE WORD WORKS
WASHINGTON, D.C.

THE WORD WORKS
P.O. Box 42164
Washington, D.C. 20015
editor@wordworksbooks.org

Cover art: Candace Hunter (chleeart)
"Northern Lights and the Sound of Billie Holiday"
Cover design: Susan Pearce
Author photograph: GlitterGuts

LCCN: 2022931902
ISBN: 978-1-944585-58-7

# Acknowledgments

Many thanks to the following people who supported me as this book was coming together: Jill Petty, for looking at these poems and telling me, "I think you have a book here"; my friends L. D. Barnes, Aurelius Raines, Andrea Change, Abdul Ali, Lisa Alvarado, and Todd Craig for your consistency and kindness. I'd also like to thank Alice Kim, Tracye Matthews, and Renaldo Hudson, the inaugural Artist for the People, for their support when I was the Poet for the People Practitioner Fellow at University of Chicago while I was pulling together the final details for this book. There are so many people being held behind bars. We cannot allow them to disappear.

I'd like to acknowledge the following journals, presses, and online publications where these poems, sometimes as earlier drafts, originally appeared:

*African American Review*: "Tangerine"
*At Length*: "Borrowed Breath"
*Bone Bouquet*: "Baltimore Starting to Sound Like Babylon"
*Cutthroat*: "Priest, the Pit Bull"
*ESPNW*: "The Two Simones"
*Ethel*: "After Andy Warhol's 'Little Race Riot'"
*FreezeRay Poetry*: "Ms. Pac Man Insists: No Sweating in High Heels"
*Glass Poetry Journal*: "High Fidelity," "Count Eggs"
*Jet Fuel Review*: "The Cut"
*Kenyon Review*: "Humidity"
*Kudzu House*: "The Simple Price of Seeds"
*Nashville Review*: "Tituba, Black Witch of Salem"
*Pinwheel Journal*: "What Bucks or Breaks"
*Poetry*: "Hip Hop Analogies"
*Poetry City*: "The Body Is Not the Bullet That Claims It"
*Poets for Living Waters*: "Oil Spill"
*RHINO*: "An Only Child"
*River Styx*: "Litany for Lieutenant Nyota Uhura," "The Urchin's Work"
*Split This Rock Poetry Database*: "FUBU"
*StorySouth*: "prestidigitation"
*Syracuse Cultural Workers Calendar 2019*: "Nina Simone"
*The Collagist*: "Inventory"

*The Feminist Wire*: "When Racism Affecting Black Girls Is Ignored"
*The Offing*: "Haiku," "Out of the Crate"
*Tayo Literary Magazine*: "Sage and Shields," "Minted," "The Suits of Our Skin"
*The Wide Shore*: "The Long Lean"
WBEZ, Chicago's National Public Radio affiliate: "A Bitter Split Silence"
*Words, Beats & Life: The Global Journal of Hip-Hop Culture*: "Because hip
hop, unlike slavery, was a choice"

And gratitude for the inclusion of these poems in the anthologies:
*Allegro & Adagio: Dance Poems, Vol. II*: "Coppelia"
*Black Lives Have Always Mattered* (2 Leaf Press, 2017): "An Open Letter
to the Voyeurs"
*Come As You Are* (Anomolous Press, 2017): "Missing TLC"
*Full Moon & Foxglove: An Anthology of Witches & Witchcraft* (Three
Drops Press, 2017): "Marie Laveau, Voodoo Queen"
*Ghost Fishing: An Eco-Justice Poetry Anthology* (University of Georgia
Press, 2018): "Taking Root"
*Nasty Women Poets: An Unapologetic Anthology of Subversive Verse*
(Lost Horse Press, 2017) and *What Saves Us: Poems of Empathy
and Outrage in the Age of Trump* (Northwestern University
Press, 2018): "Failed Spells"
*Our Girl Tuesday: An Unfurling for Dr. Margaret TG Burroughs*
(Project NIA, 2021): "Small Illuminations"
*Resisting Arrest: poems to stretch the sky* (Jacar Press, 2016): "The Suits of
Your Skins"
*The Ice Cream Poems: Reflections on Life with Ice Cream* (World
Enough Writers, 2017): "Listening to Raekwon's 'Ice Cream'"
*The Long Term: Resisting Life Sentences, Working Toward Freedom*
(Haymarket Books, 2018): "Long Division"
*Too Young, Too Loud, Too Different: Poems from Malika's Poetry Kitchen*
(Corsair, 2021): "Transcending the Bough"
*Visiting Bob: Poems Inspired by the Life and Work of Bob Dylan* (New
Rivers Press): "When Dylan Woke to George Jackson's Death"
*Voices from Leimert Park Redux* (TSEHAI/Harriet Tubman Press, 2017):
"Roscoe's with Wanda," "Refuse to Disappear"

"A Second Plate at Pearl's Place" was published as a limited edition
broadside with The Literary House Press/Rose O'Neill Literary House
at Washington College.

# Contents

## A Wall Is Just a Wall

*This is for the women, my former students,*
*and all the people who should be more visible*
*than Ellison's unforgettable protagonist.*
*You are brighter than hundreds of lights*
*burning the shadows out of all*
*the shadowy corners.*
*Remember that.*

# Transcending the Bough

*after Brittney Leeanne Williams*

To be above, to float, to rise, to crumble
within the dusk—rich, spectral
butterflies dipped in umber and kink,

pink as your palms and soles tickling
autumn leaves with tenderness
wavering like the opening of mouths.

Arc and flutter, you dance in the womb
of the sky among arteries and capillaries
reaching out as heavy branches. Understand

how roots twin that blood dance underground,
spread wider, deeper. All of you, all of us,
swimming, folding, lofty kicks in the air.

Someone will attempt to remind you,
even in this—a honeyed, cloudless
expanse—that people hid and died
in such cradles. You recall and still
levitate alive with unbound grace.

# SAY HER NAME

# When Racism Affecting Black Girls Is Ignored

*"I was overwhelmed by the thought of having to be
a black girl for the rest of my life."*
—Khadijah Costley White, *The Washington Post*

Ignoring more than obvious hands
      slicing a people in halves, more
like eminent domain cutting,
      chopping up a neighborhood
to build highways and forget,
      more like taking a shot glass
where the lip drops on a canvas
      then cutting away what rests
beyond the glass, and insisting
      that is the entire picture.
It erases all the known small faces
      then denies where sons began.
This ugly says be strong and silent,
      only to slap the deserving and reason
how she can handle anything.
      This smothering quietly descends,
keeps smiling and says,
      Wait. Behave. Your turn is coming soon.

# Inventory

*for Ciara Miller*

Standing with boxes in our arms
on the tail of August while morning
brushes our faces, we ascend in an
elevator and never let papers fool us.
Some will remind us of our descent.
Our kind are clipped, disadvantaged.
A rise rendered farfetched splits clouds
while I unpack highlighters and
a tea kettle that rests on my desk
that surrendered grit and silt to lemony
disinfectant. Coffee rings disappeared
under the now smooth surface where
my pens gather with clips and prongs
from binders. We unpack these trappings
to feel at home in a place that opened
but never welcomed us. Mentioning
our names is an act of subversion. I un-
wrap a tape dispenser without stuttering
when a woman from a few doors down
eyes my name on the office door, looks
at the lamp on the desk next to mine,
bumbles through keeping track of supplies
while her eyes shift between our thick, tall,
brown bodies in silent questioning. I ask
one question about inventory, but keep
taking stock of how many times I say
*I bought these new things. This is my office.*

# prestidigitation

each sleight of hand,
a step toward the sanitarium
the cards are always laid
to be shuffled again.
a box after stuffing myself
and sheer tights.
twitching my nose
to yank me out of a hat.
cultivates the herbs
whispers with the dead,
herself with oils, pouches,
uttered in yoruba, swahili,
dip my tongue in a diaspora,
that you may skim but
open the book of spells,
from the pages written,
make them your own,
like lipstick spread
caught in fingernails
when pains and the least
children, picket signs,
from death and deficit.
sisyphus rests on your

every spell thwarts
of worthlessness.
in order and ready
i will not be stuffed into
into glittery leotard
i am not the silent rabbit
as you pull on my ears
i am the one who
from the ground, trades
and still shields
the phrases
and spanish,
the wellspring
never dive in deep.
blow the dust away
passed down,
revamp their works
bright as your stockings
weaved through smiles
transform into raising
bank accounts, bodies
a persistence that outlasts
shoulders, so rest.

because we are magic, rules will never apply to us.

# Tituba, Black Witch of Salem

*after Maryse Condé*

Tituba, the missing hollows of your story
echo within myths and shifting details.
Centuries later, you are imagined whole.
Your name means "to atone" in Yoruba.
The books say West Indian, Arawak,
Venezuelan, anything but African.
The charges accused you of poisoning
children. Even though rye flour
bears unseen fungus spoiling bread,
cakes, and children. We will not know
the count of lashes or blows, how often
you were slapped or dunked before
you said *I am a witch. I serve the devil.*
We know this: you were the first
to confess. You walked away alive.
You were bought from bondage, fled
Salem with John, birthed a daughter
named Violet. Papers prove all of that.
Historians and scholars require some
bread crumbs, but these papers let you
imitate ether in the night and disappear.

# Litany for Lieutenant Nyota Uhura

Jet black curl whipped past her ear
lined to the rounded angle of cheek
matched to meticulous batwing
eyeliner. The red line sleek against
thigh, then calves interrupted by
black boots, but first, benediction.

In praise of communicator chirps,
in praise of the flashing monitors,
in praise of swirling chair that gave,
of her sharp lashes and poised vista
of face, enough yet not enough.
Martin Luther King, another captain
of sorts, offered his gospel. She was
to be seen, rocketing toward future.

She is the vessel that carries and delivers
when she is navigator, guide, and seer.
She is the vessel that carries and delivers
how often she is captain without title,
blamed as commander without privilege.

Question: did the Vulcan ever ask her
about what it feels like to be different?
He removed his pointy ears & brows daily,
ruffled his hair to normalcy, released his
anesthetizing grip. She takes off the wig,
but still wears herself, irreversible skin.

She becomes vessel that carries and delivers.
She serves as navigator, guide, and seer.
She is the vessel that carries and delivers
how often she is captain without title,
commander without privilege.

The conversation that never happened:
I waited for you and Sulu to cast glances
like unwritten spells, give each other
silent nods, forge some way to defect
if aliens became allies. If the captain
barked too many times and forgot
you were not just polished umber
to fantasize about in a later episode.
When you recall your surname means
Freedom, and Sulu Sea touches Asia,
when slavery and internment camps
failed to turn your ancestors to dust,
you, fourth in command, a helmsman
never called Lieutenant, could direct
a story, steer the Starship Enterprise.

# A Second Plate at Pearl's Place

A bottle of half-empty hot sauce
overlooks white plates. There
are only yellow crumbs, bits
of daylight on the smaller plate.
A larger dish serves as a pillow
that eases hunger to sleep, no
need for sugar plums or sheep.
Sweet potatoes candied into
cinnamon-laced mash, piled
next to light gold macaroni
gilded in savory cheeses.
A fork crowns greens—turnip
and mustard turned to tender
smokiness, next to a medallion
of salmon waiting to be pinned
to a tongue and savored slowly.

# Marie Laveau, Voodoo Queen

So many Maries in New Orleans
that Laveau is a maze to most.
Entire sections of newspapers
cut out, missing birth certificates
but the crypt in New Orleans
Cemetery One is real. Whites
erased free people of color
from papers. Your grave stands
clearly marked with X's as wishes,
kisses, petitions scrawled in chalk.

You might answer. You strolled,
wore white to Congo Square,
hypnotized police who meant to stop
those drums but stood stock still as
your body rolled and recalled snakes.

Damballah whispered from your back
and hips curling. Even respectable ladies
fell on their backs and writhed. Your head
covered in madras, you called testimonies,
gris-gris you gave, small pockets of power.

## Roscoe's with Wanda

Los Angeles let me have a gift.
Wanda Coleman asked me where
I wanted to go, offered to take me
on a tour that started at Viper Room
where River Phoenix crumpled
down to his last breath. I didn't want
the whole strip, but I said,
Let's go to Roscoe's Chicken & Waffles,
where we sat with our plates,
buckwheat pancakes for me, chicken & waffles
for everyone else, since I simply
craved a pilgrimage to where the rappers
like Tupac shared plates,
and I got Wanda with all her words
and her voice like a heavy opera
and I got Wanda cussing and laughing
and Wanda talking about mysteries
in poems and reading books we couldn't
afford to buy and Vallejo's *Trilce*.
The thick tangled branches of her locks,
her black jacket veined with bright
colors and flourishes of her hands on her
outstretched arms, insisting on
her worth, and she knew I saw hers,
and she saw mine, in spite of
all our lumps, without ribbons and bows.

## Two Simones

*for Simone Biles and Simone Manuel*

Miraculous is a woman—

     her dedication, her skill,

        the body that she wills

to slice air high above

     heads, land precisely.

Her shoulders squared,

     she tumbles in a leotard,

        commands every shift in muscles,

the master of limbs in her own flip.

     The twist of body

        swift and exacting.

She loops, spirals

     her way to lift arms,

        upright arch.


     Miraculous is woman

     who snaps into taut

     line as she barely

breaks the water's surface.

No engine or combustion

ignites her push, past

the others determined to make

their mark. She is focus.

Her hands clench the lip of the pool.

Her nails polished—

red, white, blue lacquer.

She covers her mouth as she bobs

in the water, then begins to weep.


These two Simones, in namesake and spirit, sever

wind and water, recall another Simone.

Nina, I wish I knew how it feels to be free.

## Nina Simone

She is syrup, pleads for sugar filling
her bowl. Deep waters rise black, thick
since she will never be watered down.
No apology ever rises from her lips
since she was so black, her heart
turned into a tender skillet to fry
lies. Cast iron cracked as she sang.

# The Urchin's Work

Between dips and swings of each syllable,
Ella knew valleys between cheery notes.
She carried a tsk tsk tsk in "A Tisket, A Tasket"
a yellow basket that seemed to be full of smiles
until it could nearly burst, and how she learned
standards. She worked until work verged on
impossible, as what unwanted children do.

Create a joy that shields them from misery,
a cocoon, a shell to block a stepfather's hands,
a mother buried, an aunt who feebly helps as she
runs numbers, a track star through Harlem.
Until Ella became delinquent, sent to Hudson,
a Sing-Sing for girls that kept her quarantined,
solitary, out of a choir reserved for white girls.

Documents say that they don't have much
on 1933, 1934, but there is a ledger bearing
a committed colored girl's name, and she ran
like a number bet on in one of her aunt's
books. The articles say Ella had no biography,
no interviews about this time upstate. Her
voice rewrote a path. She never looked back.

# Coppelia

Cecilia Sanchez loved ballet
and Coppelia was among her
favorites, so her love carried
on after the Cuban revolution
when there was ice cream.

The simple confection curled
into light scoops in a basket
that almost resembles a canoe.
A few flavors served on a given
day, strawberry and chocolate.

Available to any Cuban since
what sustains anyone in heat
and hard work are desires—
to be cool, to eat, taste sweets
and look up to see the dainty
toe shoes forming a cone's tip.
Legs of the cone lead to a tutu
like a vanilla scoop spangled
with colorful round sprinkles.

# Tangerine

**1.**

Patterned stockings under folded down
cutoffs curved in Sin-Dee's criss-crossed
lean in rapid buckled steps of bent knees.
Mid-riff leopard tied above waist, flips
brassy blonde of her wig. Alexandra holds
no cigarettes, but clear high notes, streak
of a tear, a pouch of skin that she refused.

**2.**

Alexandra smooths hair under jaw,
coupled with eyebrow arches slick
as brown leather jacket, a camel-
colored purse strap on her shoulder.
Sleek, Alexandra avoids fights, finds
release from trade in a car wash.
Foam plumes curl on the windshield.

**3.**

Urine flies in Sin-Dee's face
on a Hollywood Christmas
Eve as she solicits the next,
and silence becomes a tight
jacket over her shoulders.

Alexandra still comes back,
pulls Sin-Dee into a 24-hour
laundromat, yanks the piss-
slick clothes away to wipe
Sin-Dee clean, another pass
at innocence known by night
women, denied permits
for shame and dignity.

Alexandra unpins her halo
of polished black from rounded
stocking cap, fits the wig on
Sin-Dee's naked nylon-netted
head. Neither one speaks.
No one says prostitutes
and men who know strolls.
They do exactly what sisters do.

# FUBU

*after Solange Knowles*

I am sitting in a café with my boy
    that I have known longer than my
students have been alive, before the birth
    of his firstborn son, and the waiter
wears a tight black camisole with bright green
    beads. We smile because he is living his joy.
And how many people do that on the daily?
    And how many of us know that joy like
pink and blue hair clips latched onto flawless waves?
    And we must know some day where we are as serene
as Solange's expression always shaming Mona Lisa
    who never knew about the ice grill or paper cranes.
I find myself wanting to raise my fists like I'm in
    an elevator with my sister's husband talking sideways
but I have no sisters as blood kin. I find myself
    wanting to celebrate all the history that made me
and be a little gutter too, because once I carry
    it in my pocket, it's my slingshot and my stone
rubbed smooth by fingers and time. I find myself
    counting the sway of what I claim and protecting
it like the last medallion that could be stolen.

## Missing TLC

*for T-Boz, Left Eye, and Chilli*

I miss when girls wore big pants
and rocked many mics with men.
Girls don't even wear pants now
but I'm not mad at their onesies.

I just miss bright colors sagging
with condoms pinned to them
before respectability and agency
became buzzwords humming

on tongues that were never
smooth like the trio or quick
like Left Eye's rhyming and
not one was too proud 2 beg

or creep, a red light special
in oversized silk pajamas,
slow flow to punctuate
bounce and be up front

about not going raw and still
be fly, like a flock of three
tracking each other's motions.
Sisters with different mothers

and you just wish girls rolled
like that now, free in loose
pants, bold about latex, friends
who ask ain't that love, now?

# THE BOOM BAP

# Haiku

Lips half-pucker
surround a tiny bud,
a stud in his ear.

# High Fidelity

Cusack declares what you missed about Chicago,
       how the places with the best music and art tucked
themselves in dingy, cramped places. That's not
       romantic, it's what it was, and you ate food built
to insulate you from the hawk, air talons that cut
       your face, how the el over Damen makes
cameos in the background, how this scene is
       about love or at least amicably sharing a bed,
then having a beer because it gets cold. Why
       not talk when your love moves out as you
debate the top five loves of your life, as if
       a person could ever be the stew of the best
five albums you could hold in one hand or
       the ten best R&B songs ever recorded. People
play themselves like a tape, over and over, yet
       there is always one that throws in that one
single we forgot we knew, or never expected.
       We wait to put the needle to their etched curves,
to rewind in a deck or twist with a pencil so
       that song plays, maybe go back and find more.

## Out of the Crate

Send him each one of the old Prince
records, spread them on the living room floor,
glide over him like a needle following grooves.

# Because hip hop, unlike slavery, was a choice

Because the art classes disappeared as buildings
     burned & ashes fluttered mid-air like insurance checks,
Because the government claimed a broken window theory
     where those animals could not avoid breaking everything,
Because those animals had ancestors who knew slavery and colonialism
     like second & third languages, no ESL required,
Because Robert Moses came through the borough like
     the Expressway was his personal bushido blade,
Because mothers in the rundown apartments that survived
     collected small, flat spheres of vinyl joy,
Because they were never ashamed to dance and always
     spoke in codes & rhythms,
Because breakbeats needed to be carried on the spoken wings
     spread by emcees taking pride in making people sweat,
Because aerosol cans rendered swirls and geometric orders
     in colors imagined by God's hands brushed across dusk,
Because there were no schools that said they were civilized
     even though their lives were burglarized daily,
Because Zora Neale Hurston interviewed the last surviving slave
     brought to America, but she couldn't profit from publication,
Because Black Benjy died too young, so did DJ Scott La Rock, so did
     MC Trouble, so did Left Eye, so did B.I.G. and Tupac, need I go on?
Because Chicago made Chaka Khan, Curtis Mayfield, Muddy Waters,
     & Chess Records, & the city paints over them like fading murals,
Because there are mothers of emcees who are educators that learned
     the rhetoric of sit-ins,
Because eventually there were books and teachers that documented
     the languages and the pasts we felt obscured from textbooks,
Because people struggle to keep those books in print and others
     will spend their last on fresh kicks,
Because of the obvious sharecropping, Jim Crow, KKK, micro-aggressions,
     separate and still unequal paychecks, and misogynoir,
Because de facto segregation stay holding hands with gentrification since
     they been tight like that since they first got together,

Because black and brown people always create seismic shifts
        then give them away to allow new fissures to crack,
Because someone will always make more money off that than
        creators & the estates revert to people who ain't family,
Because slavery is still the favorite fodder of American movies
        where people love to watch suffering,
Because no matter what you buy, where you live, who you marry,
        or how much money you have, free thoughts are contained.

# Hip Hop Analogies

*after Miguel and Erykah Badu*

If you be the needle,
        I be the LP.
If you be the buffed wall,
        I be the Krylon.
If you be the backspin,
        I be the break.
If you be the head nod,
        I be the bass line.
If you be a Phillie,
        I be the razor.
If you be microphone,
        then I be palm.
If you be cipher,
        then I be beatbox.
If you be hands thrown up,
        then I be yes, yes, y'all.
If you be throwback,
        then I be remix.
If you be footwork,
        then I be uprock.
If you be turntable,
        then I be crossfader.
If you be downtown C train,
        then I be southbound Red Line.
If you be shell toes,
        then I be hoodie.
If you be freestyle,
        then I be piece book.
If you be Sharpie,
        then I be tag.
If you be boy,
        then I be girl
        who wants to
        sync samples
        into classic.

# Listening to Raekwon's "Ice Cream"

A revved up
piano loop rotates
Earl Klugh's "A Time to Love"
into tinkling ice cream trucks,
except one emcee stands on
a white truck and swings
his walking stick and recites
the familiar hook over beat.

Each series of rhymes tries
to woo a girl from around
the way who must always
remain cool, uninterested.
Even then, don't be thirsty
was a rule, another emcee
asks if her name is Erica,
calls her Black Miss America,
right, true? She offers a smirk.

Other women dance around
the truck in white ringer T's
with black trims, emblazoned
with curved capital W's, above
the letter turned symbol, each
woman is a flavor—French
Vanilla, Butter Pecan, Chocolate
Deluxe, even Caramel Sundaes.

What woman, who wants to be
cherished and whole, would be
edible, sweet, and object.

What woman wouldn't want to be
wanted, held, savored, licked and
called sweet, if one chooses to be.

# What Bucks or Breaks

watch me press
                    flat this bristling moment
                    that softens to mature bitter
this tense sugar
                    spun from shimmering refuse

absence turned solo
                    celebrating living as one, not two
                    because who needs a trap

woven from promise

                    that favors maroon ropes
                    a bloody cat's cradle—a cage

this planned life
                    puzzle out an escape
                    confinement labeled as safe

don't trust          the hands that throw you
                    on a whim, safeguarding

half-baked lies—
                    nothing that protects

or bucks             the saddle, chucks the soft rein
or breaks            i reject iron hammered to my feet

i paint these lips   brighten my face, dress in my wishes
                    ignore solicitous open palms

greet my breath

## Ms. Pac Man Insists:
## No Sweating in High Heels

Some women cannot be cornered
when choices are run, bite, or die.
So many women chased by ghosts
housed by a central cell rooted
in every scenario. Only occasional
fruit bounces its bright sugar past
too quickly. Only the most basic
simple calories sustain repetitive
tasks, because women do tedium
well, but they cannot gain weight.
Despite the stalking and killing her
kind, or consumption that shrinks
others like her to fleeting blip, she
applies eye shadow and lipstick,
fixes a bow like a rose on her head,
runs like hell behind walls through
sharp turns and tunnels, while not
sweating and wearing high heels.

## The Long Lean

I used to have people that I called after midnight,
a sway of voice into voice, steady breath trekking
deep into the night. I pray for sleep until daylight.
Dispel dark solitude and hear traces of waking life
as absence ebbs in the sun. I deserve a cradle
into closed lids with the deep rise and fall of chest
into dawn, the occasional clutch out of nightmares
that jar more than any horror movie. In a space
where unrolled tapestries might drift me into sleep,
I break sharp corners of dreams, watch chunks
crumble into ether within the cosmos of skull.
The people who love you send cards, text, call
during the day. I avoid staring into computer
screen bent on insomnia. My job is sleep,
making it through the long lean of the night.

## The Cut

A chair spins you straight into the mirror's view.
The stylist shears inches of hair, tenderly prunes
your hair into a cap. Think Joan of Arc, '80s pop star
when you have felt what once twisted around neck.
Shoulders become a cape where sweat and wind lift
heat away from the skin. Fingers raise the hair away
where there is something like freedom from weight,
the comb, and the blow dryer. Wake up feeling like
this head is a light, feathery glory that should know
fingers lingering and wrapping around its almost curls.

## Prayer Box

Plop of a fat tear hits the yoga mat.
You could swear everyone heard it
over the instructor's soft dictates.
A few more drops wet your face as
you straighten out of a pose and roll
up the mat like a thick scroll padded
with words instead of spongy foam.
You excuse yourself. Class continues.

Outside, you sit on a bench. An arc
of grief speeds toward the billowing
silk of barely clinging calm and rends
across a face in a downpour of snot
and weeping. A friend assures you
how asanas release and hurt seeps
out. You nod into a used tissue.

The instructor, light as a pixie, appears.
When she touches your shoulder, a tiny
box of a lidded charm winks on her wrist.
You ask. She explains it is a prayer box.
You want a row of them to encircle
your arm, wishes dangling so you can
fasten one above your dead mother's hand.

# An Only Child

I was almost a never-been child.
My grandmother planted wishes
that would not grow inside her.
Unformed fingers and toes,
language of ligaments.

Then, a child with a circus
turning to the left of his spine.
Lamps radiating lines in his dark
pupils. This was finally no could-be
child. My father was a child, soft
calcium, a thickening murmur in bones,
dimpled knees smirking on each leg.

My father held a cannon of laughter
growing wide and deadly in his chest
each day. His blast still inert, aimless,
only child touched by ether brothers,
dust sister—almost-were children, but
he was a child long enough to pull
my brother and me from never-been land.

He is,   so we are—not could-be, almost-
were, nor never-been. His thoughts tumble
through borrowed breaths when syringe sunk
like a focused anchor or his knuckles hatch-
marked purple on my mother. My almost-
were uncles and could-be aunt raced toward
tickertape of first breath, slowed, stumbled,
no cries, stopped. A hovering committee

circling of unborn as I began counting the rise
of ribs and how many arms could have held
me as a child. Their faces set in the relief
of my grandmother's profile, while my father
quit but kept drawing breath, a gnawing frost.

## Count Eggs

Break an egg, sing its yolk
into this yellow undulation.
The bowl steadies its rocking
until the stirring stills. Avoid
crying into this breakfast
beginning. Count eggs, while
there is no actual count. A clock
nestled beneath your navel
conceals how many are hiding,
who might stop its hands, start
some other timetable within, or
how to carry, no expelled lining
as you turn into oven, or cradle.

# The Simple Price of Seeds

Seeds are one currency that remains
unspent until they root in pockets of soil
split hard hulls and offer exchanges
of what fills the stomachs without labs
or stocks exacted. The trade of seeds
is a bartering of coins that could save
us from our own small preferences.
Seeds host lost possibilities, found
plants—the cure and the balm.

# Taking Root

for Wangari Maathai (1940-2011)

In the valleys and forests of Kenya, she stood,
stalwart as a tree. She knew what trees could
give. She remembered the land with fig trees
untouched. She recalled beads of frogs' eggs
glistening on the banks of rivers, water clear
and bubbling, before the crops of tea cut down
broad trunks like mere stubble on a man's face.

Do not assume the rudimentary rise of branches
only mirrors the roots adumbrating into routes
underground. The unthinking forget the concert
between soil held in place, shade that protects
the living who remember the dead, water gurgling
to the air that bubbles and lifts leaves and blades
of grass. The trees boom a chorus of quiet drums.

When her people saw the rivers dwindle to trickle,
and topsoil was swept away, and even tea failed
to thrive, the dazed wonder of malnutrition pointed
its gaze at adopting crops like customs that never
matched the sustenance that grew as it should
before strangers insisted this is the way. We need
not see every layer to know what we might see.

She knew that losing the trees was more than trees
in parks and public forests, those lungs breathing
in Kenya and the Congo. So, when bulldozers came
and pangas were brandished, she planted seedlings,
and taught women to plant trees like the crops
they already knew. They stopped demolitions,
and men more interested in pockets than breath.

When the planting of trees and protesting occurs,
a common movement occurs, the act of taking root.

# Oil Spill

When the knife enters and rotates,
hemorrhage spumes into currents.
Black blood tinged red laps pulse
into blue flushed with viscous night
clouds water.  Fish bellies, obscured
white, still gills, stiff as clotted feathers
weighed down. No touch stems the flow.
Teacup ships float in a flood. The knife
turns deeper when a bell jar fails to pump
a gulf to safety.  No eyes soak up miles
gone, cloaked in endless black scalloped
into oily deserts abandoned by fishermen,
tourists. No one ventures to dead beaches.

While company town founders and barons
bedeck bone china with organic vegetables
and folded hand-woven cotton napkins, oil,
in their dreams, raises profit margin buoys
and glazes salads with extra virgin olive.
Slick does not stain everyone's water
glass, just ones that have to twist the tap.

# Borrowed Breath

The sky, an invisible cage that fetters
air with toxic bars from acronyms,
opens and pulls back its lone lip.
Blackbirds assume a canary's fate.

Fumes creep into lungs small as walnuts,
nip the alveoli, roll the eyes into
final descent—a chorus of tumbling on land,
not just a clutch of folded feathers,
but diving flocks, like sparks.

There is no bullet fragment to extract
from flesh, unseen parts per million,
a kind of counting most don't fathom
unless playing the lottery. Don't
they know this is another ticket?

# Humidity

City summers will make you plead,
wipe away the act weighing down
your skin. Wait for the silk overhead
to rip open and pour its torrents
in threads suspended in mid-air
before predictable crash corrupts
the concrete with puddles. This heat
clings to your skin harder and closer
than a lover's funk creeping out
of still unwashed skin. You beg
for the whisper of this water. Dream
on the patter cooling like an open
refrigerator or icy crust of snowflake,
the rapid death of frost on your cheek
in ice-glazed months when you wish
for heat like some sort of lost savior.

# A WALL IS JUST A WALL

# After Andy Warhol's "Little Race Riot"

the man in a straw fedora is not the center
of the reproduced photograph, black and blue
like Louis Armstrong's plaintive query,

black and white like america being simple
about every damn ingredient that fills its pot,
often stirred by black hands. the man in a straw

fedora is being chased to the margins. two
officers chase him, but the german shepherds
are central, every movement in a country

where darker bodies stand down with empty
raised hands, and some will write, photograph,
and paint the origami sharply unfolded in this

silk screened pair. surely, someone's cousins are
in the background where dogs are hardly restrained,
and the protagonists on the right side of this story

will be subjects, fodder for weapons and auctions
still on repeat, the same photo rendered again
to replicate how american horrors are great,
and how any riot rising is laughably not little.

# Sage and Shields

*for Shameeka Dream*

On Baltimore's North Street,
lacing the line of officers
with a smoldering sage,
no riot erupted in your face.

A white line of gentle smoke,
your scarf pointed toward
them, a compass to cleansing.

You walked one end
of the line to the other
and embodied breeze.

Black, green, yellow
bracelets on wrists—
land, light, and skin
remembered.

Your lids lowered
in prayers that every
head under helmet

and shield finds
indecipherable.
Hair pulled back.

Water in your left
hand, another way
to cleanse and honor

the dead. Officer shields
held up high so each
man stood unknowing.

You summoned.
They will answer to
another type of army.

# Baltimore Starting to Sound Like Babylon

*...they made them gats.*
*They got some shit that'll*
*blow out our backs*
*from where they stay at...*
—Andre 3000 on Outkast's "Babylon"

The planes are circling Baltimore.
        We could say they are rehearsing
for other cities, other dead caught
        in a profile that race gives finality
as a fortune, and we could get used
        to helicopters whirring near
our windows, and crushing tank
        treads punish the worn streets.

We could even say that placards
        and broken windows meant more
and we could say that changed law
        almost as quick as a spine snapped.

Once what's on paper changes,
        ask what protects us from circling
steel predators overhead.  While we
        watch the news, what flashing blip
distracts us from loaded catapult
        drawn and aimed at living rooms
where we could be alive, then gone.

# Minted

*for Sandra Bland*

When your life drags in front of you,
raw meat on a rope along the ground,
you are less concerned about the dirt.

There is no camera that can protect.
Any daily routine becomes rattled
by doubt and a swift officer's hold

that ensures you will never come
home. Pressed cuffs of your suit
and straight coif fold like bones

thrown to the ground, oxygen
flattened from your lungs. Fault
is sharply pressed between slats

that used to be your life, adamant
in value, minted in video footage.
You thanked a person recording

your last living appearance, final
moment of insistent breath choked.
Women disappear and churches burn.

# When Dylan Woke to George Jackson's Death

*Sometimes I think this whole world*
*is one big prison yard.*
*Some of us are prisoners.*
*The rest of us are guards.*
—Bob Dylan

That August 1971 morning, Dylan could have been rattled
alive and shaken with everything the Panthers could have
told him, and Angela Davis's bold soft-spoken tenets raking
across his grief when he lifted his pen and pressed letters
into words on paper. Some blues fell out of his grief to say
Lord, Lord because the prison guards shot Jackson to death
bleeding and without a single weapon. The ballad closed
on every verse that a life sentence is not equal to $70 stolen
much less his life that George never lived on his knees, so
Dylan echoed what the black folks knew. He would not bow.

# A Bitter, Split Silence

Gathered behind yellow tape,
police stand much taller than
children who typically bend limbs
to race one other, shoot basketball,

the vacant lot where girls ran footballs
with boys. Tonight is not that routine.
Officers guard the cordoned street
and the neighboring lot—thick grass

fresh and still growing. Two tried to
get children to talk. Their faint shudders
dodge questions that guaranteed no safety.

Tonight, a young man in a foot race
days ago failed to outpace the stone
burrowing into his arm, but he lives.

Miss Adams does not stutter. She points
out overgrown lots where houses stood.
No child is more special than another.
Her nephew Christopher Lattin, lost at

Stroger, same hospital where a lean sprinter
heals tonight. Again, the shooters go free,
yet these children waver. Quiet floods July
sky that got dark so quick, but not before

an ice cream truck inched toward the block.
Its sugary tinkling song hushed and turned away.
Kids who ran to it for frozen joys are gone.
Funerals stay unplanned tonight. No one

memorializes childhood or resistant
grass that bears witness. A bitter split
silence falls where houses used to breathe,
while police look for fallen casings.

# The Body Is Not the Bullet That Claims It

The scream is peeled from myths
of banshees a too familiar chorus,
folded staccato. Newspapers confuse
this as the only sound—as if reports
claim there is no music, no giggles,
no birthdays, no soul claps, no moans,

only compounded griefs released
from an opening torn by projectile
and velocity erupting with fevered
ripping of a ragged mouth in body.

Bullets have always been justification
to take away a sense of human, to say
the dead bare claws, even as a mother
emits a blade of high, hollow pain.

# An Open Letter to the Voyeurs

I keep trying to write a sentence, simple and clear, but I keep writing the beginnings of poems that process the electricity and extinguishing of human charges, a persistent black light, a startling series of resistant sparks. The flashing clouds of shots fired puncture the flesh that we know, pinned down to this death language that they want us to speak like our first tongue, but it is a language without tone, a tongue of decaying then dissipating spirit. There are days when the songs of my dead seem to be the only notes that people trace with fascination, a morbid savoring that ignores anything that helped someone like me live. This body of mine is alive, a product of being hugged, shared laughter, the dismantling of so-called textbooks. When you break me down to a product that purchases so many consumable goods, cuts down my life and blames me for having babies so young, there is some equation where the pennies I make add up to someone else's vacation in Antibes, and their children might reference it in an easily published poem. My poems must talk about the anglings of flesh in cell phone cameras, once breathing, then red, still.

I must be fascinated with my own death, subsumed in grief I did not build. This sort of death is not old age, diet, smoking, alcohol, or drugs. This sort of death falls short of cancer, diabetes, and heart disease. It is not an accident. Accidents require fewer bullets. Accidents are not just that call that startles you out of sleep. Accidents are never systematic, repetitive, and unloaded daily. Accidents do not extinguish parents in front of children, nor do they swing pendulum toward a skin that catches a glinting sun in a whole other character.

No, this is the deliberate swing of phone books, pulled triggers, and drop hammers. This is the dragging of bodies into warehouses to say, "Look at how they kill each other."

This is the shaking of heads that say look at their report cards, sex lives, and past records. This is the editors who will ask you can they publish another poem about your dead because your nihilism is spiced just right with hot sauce from your bag and some peach cobbler from the black restaurants that don't survive in rejuvenated neighborhoods. This is the paean that no one wants to find in a hymnal because the chorus points at who is holding the gun, instead of the dead on the floors, in graves, and left on the streets of America, a country known for jagged hurts waiting in its buck knife. Don't expect less from a two-sided blade ever.

This is a history wired, routed to eliminate, dim any charge that jumps clear off grid. Some seem to forget how I am a daily observer of electricity.

# Long Division

How many decades of calendars reveal what is starkly plantation? How wide green fields are within the walls. Floors polished spotless as walls sag with layers of paint older than me. It is endless counting for the regimented lines to meals, walks within gated yards for men on crutches, infinite uniforms to wash, dawns and nights, but time hangs, looms for acts committed so quickly (or not). Time lassoes anchors to their necks—most of those necks are dark inheritors of knotted rope legacies. Moments in a classroom with a broken window remind me of younger students, but they are men, men who are fathers and uncles, in a place where books are minted as rare capital. They think. I am sitting at a table full of black and brown men in a classroom which never happens outside these walls. The wrongness of prisons and schools collide. The grand execution of an intentional mistake, and intentional means a deliberate act, not an accident. An accident is not orderly rows or an easy rhythm to follow. Recovering from accidents is easier. The frittering away of lives behind concrete and bars punches into registers, rings incessantly—calculated yet incalculable.

# Failed Spells

For almost four years, I lived in Rod Serling's hometown,
and the sun would disappear and stay gone, as if East
Seattle or lower Alaska claimed me. All the days circled
drab as bus stops, but that quiet sounded nothing like
the hush after election day, almost as quiet as pipeline
contracts and murderers acquitted by mistrials
or paid leaves, death older than all. Remember we can't
drink oil, and oil makes money, but no one can eat either,
even if pennies rest their tinny savor on tongues like blood.

The sidewalks of Washington Heights and Brooklyn feel
solid, too damned quiet before spray painted swastikas,
ripped hijabs, and burned churches can be tallied. What
can be said to the man with access to the button when he
is more concerned with tweets? He'd kill birds for a profit,
collateral damage. What country is this? The land where
company towns and segregation threaded the railroads
and cotton fields, but this same earth, this cursed and
blessed soil is where we say no. The fields where promises
of powerful fools will bow some, but promises are destined
to go brittle, break into failed spells that will be uttered again.

# The Suits of Your Skins

*for Ciara, David, and Perre*

A simple grey suit behind glass.
I stood close enough breathless.
The shooter was almost this close
to Harvey Milk, a man he dropped.

Bullet holes in the once white
shirt surround faded sepia
stains that cling to frayed
fabric. There is more than one
hole. Black people know there
is always more than one hole.

There is more than one black
child standing beside me.
I hold my breath for three
inhales, three exhales for
each because their heads
come at the cheapest price.

And the whispers will say
they deserved restraints,
the beatings were expected,
they were due for death.

And what to tell the black girl
when the magazines erase her
one page at a time. She could
disappear and no one will put
her lost body in a headline.
Her limbs anathema to the news.

And what to tell the two queer
black boys who could be my sons,
who could be beaten into misshapen

blood melons and left like loosely tied
garbage bags. What to tell the black
children who would be told to never
reach for anything—not a cell phone,
a wallet, a bb gun, a water pistol,
a dashboard, a doorknob, rights.

And what to tell the white classmates
who do not understand experiments
are carried out on outcasts first. (Say *stop*
because you do not want to say *I am next*.)

And what to tell all the students when
assault vehicles click out of stockpiles
and occupy the streets with tear gas.

Yes, I am looking at a jacket, pants, and shirt
wrinkled after a long day at work, then death.
This suit of a dead white gay man on a stamp
and immortalized in film. The three huddled
around me mean more than a suit for a man
that people still pity. I look still as I tremble
inside for the three students around me—
each of them a brilliant burst just opening
that could be extinguished and only folks
like me will canonize them. I echo my loves.

I write you down, sketch your stamps,
remember your jokes, insist the suits
of your skins are not for idle display.

## Priest, the Pit Bull

Priest, the pit bull, greeted me the first day
he moved into my building. His tan fur shining
as he wiggled. At least three quarters of his body
wagged when I patted his head and stroked
his sinewed back. His mouth, open and panting,
made up at least half of his face, full of teeth,
but gently smiling.

I called his name, shouted to him
and the other neighbors when I heard his
ticking claws on hallway tiles. I'd laugh about
Ron O'Neal playing his namesake in *Superfly*.

He'd quietly trot over and let me pet him.
He never needed a leash. Nothing felt like fear
gnashing its teeth into the back of my hand.

I make it a habit to return kindness to other living
beings, even when the world marks them as dangerous.

# Small Illuminations

I.
Albert is a gentle tower.
His arms arched over tabletop
like bridge beams or girders.

Even if he does not understand
everything he reads, he smiles
like a good kid, like the kid he
probably was 30-some-years
ago when he was in the wrong
car with the wrong people
at the wrong time that he will
never get back.


II.
The attention to detail
borders on flawless.
Unscuffed white sneakers,
perfected lined fades
tucked under precisely
folded skullies immaculate
with what you got as a
clean, hard-fought pride.


III.
One week, I bring
crisp folders,
a bundle of sharpened pencils
with full pink erasers, round
and soft as a doll's blush.
They rub away small errors,
clearing smudges from a page
like an actual correction.

IV.
I look for Albert's easy grin first
when I walk into the concrete block
classroom. Locked in the education
building, relieved that the broken
window denies the cold like a plea.
One brother in blues with thermal sleeves
peeking out of the dull faded ocean
of cloth arching over his torso.

A cellmate hands me the slightly worn,
safeguarded, staple-bound book of poems—
the signature resolute and matching letters
of a poet's name who strolled into prison
like a mother without fear of any child.

Margaret Burroughs—more than a decade
since she left the cell of her body. I clutch
her poems knowing how they passed
from her hands like a prayer. We both smile—
small illuminations in a dark hell—when
the cellmate says Albert wanted you to have this.
He got transferred. He knew you'd keep it safe.

# Clear Plastic Bag

When you visit, you forfeit privacy.
Carry a pen, ID, a clean notebook,
a folder full of poems. You juggle
them in your grasp, against forearm
until you assign heavier books.

Acquiescence arrives as a clear stadium
bag with black nylon straps. A guard
who sifted through every page before
merely pokes between notebook
and paperbacks, shuffles a few pages.

The officer barely glances at the words.
The routine starts with
take off your shoes,
then touch socks to cold tile,
the pat down
from waist to pants cuffs,
show the top of your panties,
lift underwire in your bra.
That might be enough.

You cannot wear gloves or scarves in winter,
and never large metal earrings. You carry as
little as possible, where a little gets heavier
as you pass through ancient clanging gates.

The bag is exposed, much like your body
swaddled in extra layers of clothing to get
past the guards, to share the weight of words.

# Refuse to Disappear

*the sunsets eye saw*
*are cluttered*
*with the bones of these ashes*
*time is the fire*
*in which we burn*

    —from Eric Priestley's "Rage"

the dawns i see
burst with
ghosts of exhumed ruins
plans are murderers
in which we disappear

we are bent to follow
the maze where wall
turns into wall after wall
and we keep turning
when we should climb

look over walls
it gets more difficult
to make them too high
or hide a point of exit
time may burn and i
refuse to disappear

# About the Author

Tara Betts is the author of *Break the Habit* and *Arc & Hue*. In addition to her work as a teaching artist and mentor for young poets, she has taught at several universities, including Rutgers University and University of Illinois-Chicago, and at Stateville Prison via Prison + Neighborhood Arts Project. She is currently the Inaugural Poet for The People Practitioner Fellow at University of Chicago. Tara is also the Poetry Editor at *The Langston Hughes Review* and founder of the nonprofit organization The Whirlwind Learning Center on Chicago's South Side.

# About the Artist

Candace Hunter (chlee) creates collage, paintings, installations and performance art. Plainly, she tells stories. Through the use of appropriated materials from magazines, vintage maps, cloth, various re-used materials, she offers this new landscape of materials back to the viewer with a glimpse of history and an admiration of the beautiful. A highly respected artist in the Midwest, chlee recently received the 2021 3Arts Next Level Award, the 2020 Tim and Helen Meier Family Foundation Award, the 2016 3Arts Award, and she was honored by the Diasporal Rhythms Collective in 2020. chlee is represented exclusively by the Stella Jones Gallery.

## About The Word Works

Since its founding in 1974, The Word Works has steadily published volumes of contemporary poetry and presented public programs. Its imprints include The Washington Prize, The Tenth Gate Prize, The Hilary Tham Capital Collection, and International Editions.

Monthly, The Word Works offers free literary programs in its Café Muse and Poets vs. the Pandemic series. Word Works programs have included "In the Shadow of the Capitol," a symposium and archival project on the African American intellectual community in segregated Washington, D.C.; the Gunston Arts Center Poetry Series; the Poet Editor panel discussions at The Writer's Center; Master Class work-shops; and writing retreats in Tuscany, Italy.

As a 501(c)3 organization, The Word Works has received awards from the National Endowment for the Arts, the National Endowment for the Humanities, the D.C. Commission on the Arts & Humanities, the Witter Bynner Foundation, Poets & Writers, The Writer's Center, Bell Atlantic, the David G. Taft Foundation, and others, including many generous private patrons.

An archive of artistic and administrative materials in the Washington Writing Archive is housed in the George Washington University Gelman Library. The Word Works is a member of the Community of Literary Magazines and Presses and its books are distributed by Small Press Distribution.

wordworksbooks.org

# Other Books in the Hilary Tham Capital Collection

Nathalie Anderson, *Stain*
Mel Belin, *Flesh That Was Chrysalis*
Carrie Bennett, *The Land Is a Painted Thing*
Doris Brody, *Judging the Distance*
Sarah Browning, *Whiskey in the Garden of Eden*
Grace Cavalieri, *Pinecrest Rest Haven*
Nikia Chaney, *to stir &*
Cheryl Clarke, *By My Precise Haircut*
Christopher Conlon, *Gilbert and Garbo in Love*
      & *Mary Falls: Requiem for Mrs. Surratt*
Donna Denizé, *Broken Like Job*
W. Perry Epes, *Nothing Happened*
David Eye, *Seed*
Bernadette Geyer, *The Scabbard of Her Throat*
Elizabeth Gross, *this body / that lightning show*
Barbara G. S. Hagerty, *Twinzilla*
Lisa Hase-Jackson, *Flint & Fire*
James Hopkins, *Eight Pale Women*
Donald Illich, *Chance Bodies*
Brandon Johnson, *Love's Skin*
Thomas March, *Aftermath*
Marilyn McCabe, *Perpetual Motion*
Judith McCombs, *The Habit of Fire*
James McEwen, *Snake Country*
Miles David Moore, *The Bears of Paris*
      & *Rollercoaster*
Kathi Morrison-Taylor, *By the Nest*
Tera Vale Ragan, *Reading the Ground*
Michael Shaffner, *The Good Opinion of Squirrels*
David Allen Sullivan, *Black Butterflies over Baghdad*
Maria Terrone, *The Bodies We Were Loaned*
Hilary Tham, *Bad Names for Women* & *Counting*
Barbara Ungar, *Charlotte Brontë, You Ruined My Life*
      & *Immortal Medusa*
Jonathan Vaile, *Blue Cowboy*

Rosemary Winslow, *Green Bodies*
Kathleen Winter, *Transformer*
Michele Wolf, *Immersion*
Joe Zealberg, *Covalence*

CPSIA information can be obtained
at www.ICGtesting.com
Printed in the USA
JSHW020127281022
32216JS00004B/22